THE
SECRET
SEX
LIVES
OF
ANIMALS

THE
SECRET
SEX
LIVES

OF
ANIMALS

DAVID LAMBERT AND THE DIAGRAM GROUP

Sterling Publishing Co., Inc.
New York

Library of Congress Cataloging-in-Publication Data Available

10 9 8 7 6 5 4 3 2 1

Published by Sterling Publishing Co., Inc.
387 Park Avenue South, New York, N.Y. 10016

Created by Diagram Visual Information Limited
195 Kentish Town Road, London, NW5 2JU, England

© 2005 Diagram Visual Information Limited

Distributed in Canada by Sterling Publishing
c/o Canadian Manda Group, 165 Dufferin Street
Toronto, Ontario, Canada M6K 3H6

Written by	David Lambert
	and the Diagram Group
Production	Richard Hummerstone
Art director	Anthony Atherton
Picture research	Neil McKenna
Artists	Kathy McDougall, Coral Mula,
	Pavel Kostal, Graham Rosewarne

Printed in China

ISBN 1-4027-2837-9

For information about custom editions, special sales, premium and
corporate purchases, please contact Sterling Special Sales Department
at 800-805-5489 or specialsales@sterlingpub.com.

Introduction

★ A man meets a woman and together they create another human being.

★ Sometimes the woman gives birth to twins or triplets and up to 15 children have been born at once!

★ Whales do it upright, heads out of water, and the female takes over a year to give birth to her child.

★ The female praying mantis eats her lover after they have joined.

★ Both male and female cuttlefish die after union, and the children are born orphans.

★ A female mussel produces 25 million children at a single birth (that's more than the population of New York).

★ Worms are both male and female, so when they seek a partner they lie head to tail, and both enjoy the parentage of their offspring.

The living world has countless ways of enjoying sex and producing the next generation: this book shows some of them!

Includes an index color-coded by animal type.

Contents

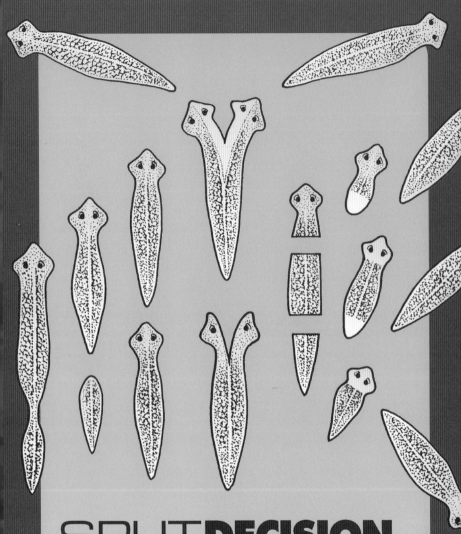

SPLIT**DECISION**

Most species of flatworm reproduce by union with another flatworm, but the most common species have the power to regenerate themselves if they are cut into two. If the head is split two heads can form and split from each other. If a flatworm is cut into sections along its width, each section will develop whatever part is lacking and continue a separate life.

500 SEXES

A slime mold seen on rotting wood could be mistaken for a branching fungus yet it is neither fungus, nor animal, nor plant. Even odder, one slime mold's spores can produce eight kinds of sex cell that can combine in various ways. Other species have yet more kinds. Altogether, more than 500 sexes figure in the weird world of slime molds.

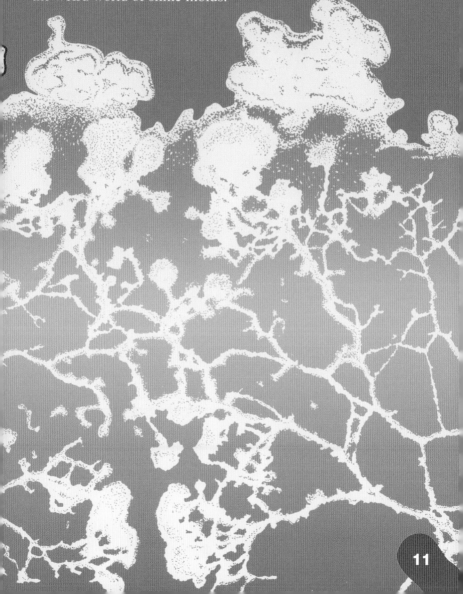

SPAGHETTI **SEA**

Twice a year, palolo worms of deep Pacific waters shed billions of male and female segments resembling spaghetti. So many writhe to the surface that people say a stick dropped into the sea stays upright at first. After eggs and sperm break out of the segments, the fertilized eggs sink back to the ocean floor.

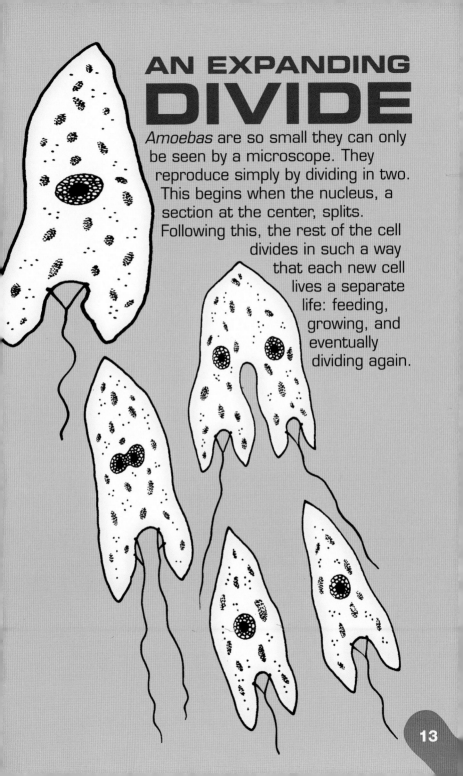

AN EXPANDING
DIVIDE

Amoebas are so small they can only be seen by a microscope. They reproduce simply by dividing in two. This begins when the nucleus, a section at the center, splits. Following this, the rest of the cell divides in such a way that each new cell lives a separate life: feeding, growing, and eventually dividing again.

SAUSAGE MACHINE

A tapeworm head hooks into an animal's gut and sprouts a string of flat "sausages." Each has male and female sex organs producing fertilized eggs, which are later passed out with the host animal's feces. Some tapeworms sprout more than four miles of segments, producing two billion eggs.

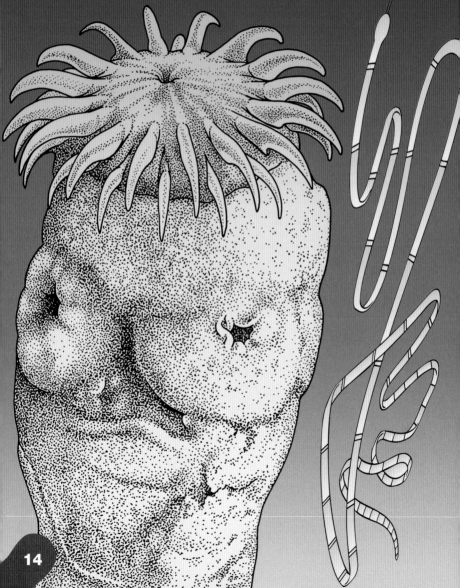

SEX CHANGE

A bacterium found in certain jointed-legged
invertebrates can make their offspring male,
female, or infertile. In one kind of woodlouse, for
example, the bacterium *Wolbachia* turns
developing males into *Wolbachia*-infected
females. Subsequent breeding of such woodlice
helps *Wolbachia* to spread.

AEROBATICS

Male ruby-throated hummingbirds woo females with fast U-shaped flights. Starting higher than a house, the tiny creatures dive groundward at top speed. At the last moment they turn, and zoom up again. A female mates with a male who performs fine aerobatics or controls a food-rich territory. The pea-sized eggs she lays are among the world's smallest birds' eggs.

SOLO SEX

Many kinds of male and female creatures occasionally stimulate their own sex organs. Some do this indirectly: during the breeding season a red deer stag may masturbate by rubbing his antlers through grass. This is enough to make him ejaculate, releasing sperm as if mating with a female. He may repeat this more than once later in the same day.

GAY ADÉLIES

Same-sex sex occurs in many animals. Sometimes two male Adélie penguins bow to each other like a courting couple. One lies down and lifts his tail like a female ready to be mated. The other mounts and copulates. The two then swap over. Incidentally, like most birds, penguins lack a penis. Each sex's genital tract ends in a simple opening in the body.

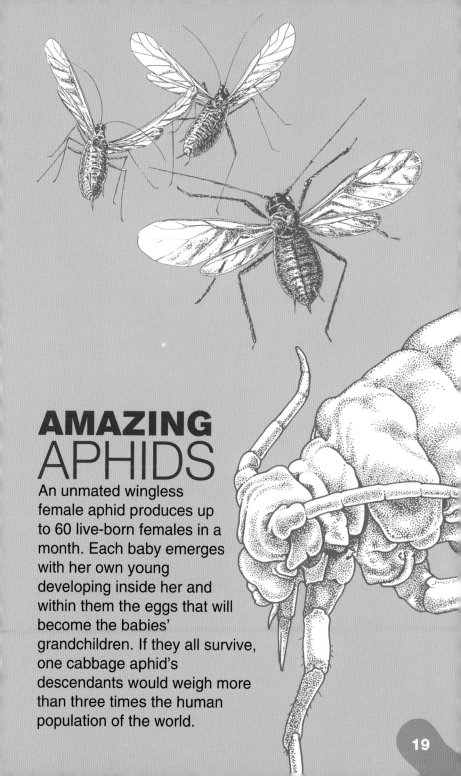

AMAZING
APHIDS

An unmated wingless female aphid produces up to 60 live-born females in a month. Each baby emerges with her own young developing inside her and within them the eggs that will become the babies' grandchildren. If they all survive, one cabbage aphid's descendants would weigh more than three times the human population of the world.

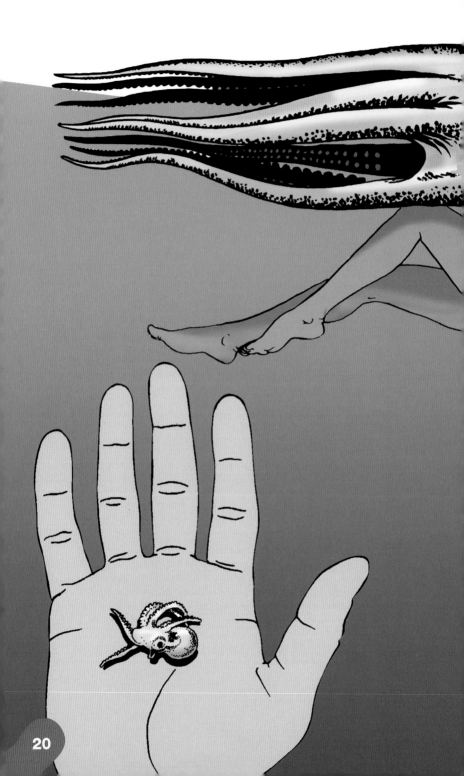

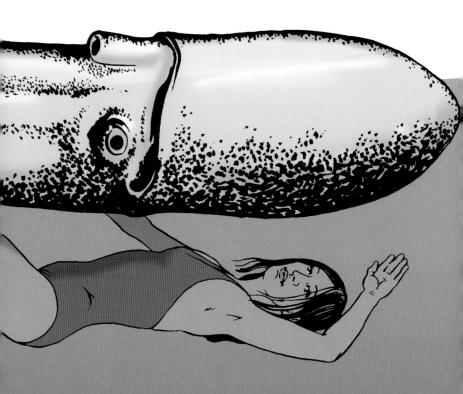

AN ODD MATCH

In many species the males and females are different sizes. For example in humans, men are usually taller and bigger than women. The blanket octopus is an extreme example of this difference in size. The male blanket octopus is a tiny creature only about 1 inch (2.5 cm) long. The female blanket octopus is a huge 6 feet (1.8 m) long and 40,000 times heavier! Male blanket octopuses never argue with their wives.

MMM YUMMY!

The mantis is an insect that preys on other insects. The female will sometimes devour her own mate during intercourse, but the male is able to continue mating with her even after his head and brains have been eaten!

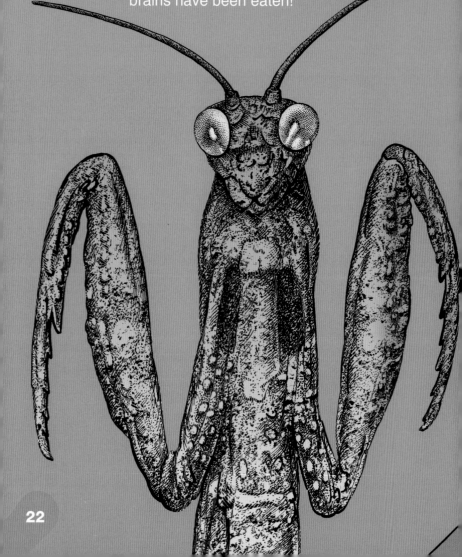

THE WHEEL
OF LOVE

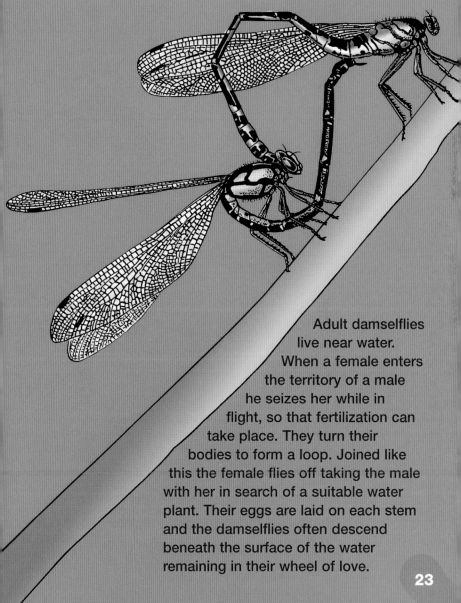

Adult damselflies
live near water.
When a female enters
the territory of a male
he seizes her while in
flight, so that fertilization can
take place. They turn their
bodies to form a loop. Joined like
this the female flies off taking the male
with her in search of a suitable water
plant. Their eggs are laid on each stem
and the damselflies often descend
beneath the surface of the water
remaining in their wheel of love.

LITTLE
TITCH

Green spoon worms start life neither male nor female. A larva that does not soon meet a female becomes a female. A larva that meets a grown female becomes a male, but 200,000 times tinier than she is. If they were people he would be the size of her fingertip. The midget male spends his life in her reproductive tract just fertilizing eggs.

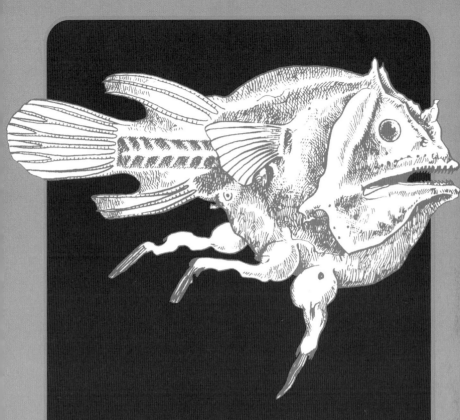

TILL DEATH
DO US PART

The male angler fish is very small compared to the female. By biting her flesh he becomes attached to her body. His mouth fuses with her skin, and the fishes' bloodstreams become connected. In this way females have been known to have several males merged into their bodies. Once joined the male starts to degenerate until he shrivels up and simply becomes a source of sperm.

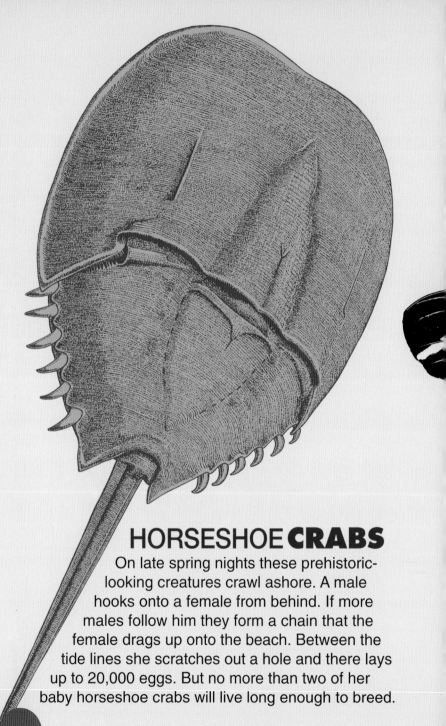

HORSESHOE **CRABS**

On late spring nights these prehistoric-looking creatures crawl ashore. A male hooks onto a female from behind. If more males follow him they form a chain that the female drags up onto the beach. Between the tide lines she scratches out a hole and there lays up to 20,000 eggs. But no more than two of her baby horseshoe crabs will live long enough to breed.

ZEBRA BUTTERFLIES

Male zebra longwing butterflies can detect a female still developing inside her chrysalis. Sometimes one tears a hole in its spiny wall and mates with her before even her wings are fully formed. He will also smear her with a scent that rival males detest. This way no other males will try to fertilize her eggs.

MIDAIR **MATING**

Fast-flying, sickle-winged birds
called chimney swifts feed, drink,
gather nest materials, and
maybe even sleep on the wing.
They mate in midair too. While
the female holds her wings
spread wide apart, the male
descends upon her back, his
own wings held almost
vertical. The pair then
glide for the brief time
that he takes to transfer
sperm to her.

HOOKED

Two fossils reveal the strange courtship of a pair of tiny sharks that lived 325 million years ago. Both evidently died while the female was biting a long, hook-shaped fine spine jutting out above the male's head. Such spines earned this kind of shark its scientific name *Falcatus*, meaning "hook" or "sickle."

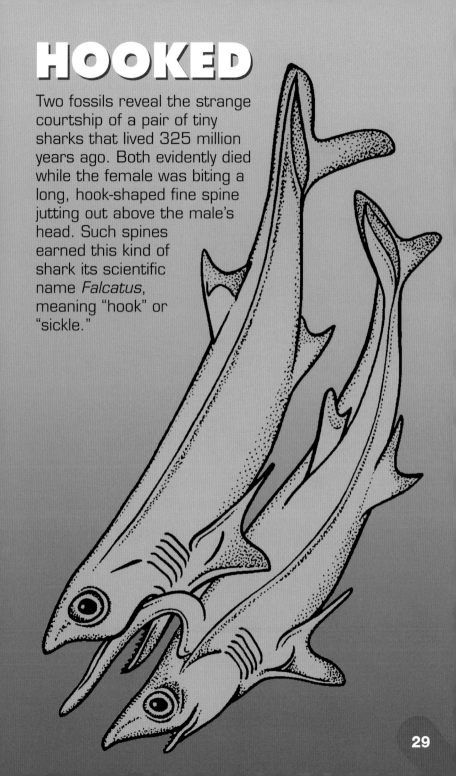

FLASHING
FIREFLIES

Each firefly species gives off flashes of light in its own way to attract a mate. In Malaysian creeks male fireflies of one species gather in their thousands to produce a striking light display. After dark, they gradually synchronize their flashes until whole trees glow, darken, and glow again as if adorned with fairy lights alternating on and off.

FAITHFUL VOLES

Once mated with a female, a male prairie vole stays passionately true. Far from eyeing other females, he attacks them. Such fidelity is rare in animals: in male prairie voles the bond arises largely from the act of mating, which lets loose an "aggression" hormone in the male's brain. A mated male fights any vole he meets except his partner.

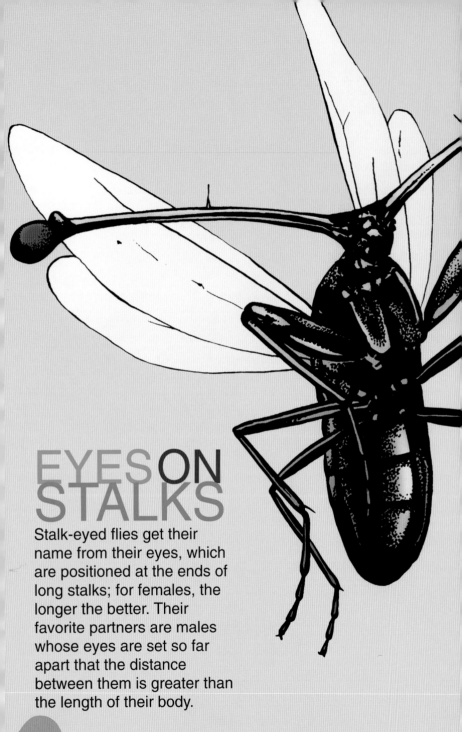

EYES ON STALKS

Stalk-eyed flies get their name from their eyes, which are positioned at the ends of long stalks; for females, the longer the better. Their favorite partners are males whose eyes are set so far apart that the distance between them is greater than the length of their body.

FOOD OF
LOVE

Female scorpion flies prefer to mate with males who offer the tastiest, meatiest presents. Males who offer dead crickets win lots of matings. Males who only offer their own saliva as tidbits win fewer matings. Males with nothing to offer win the fewest matings of all.

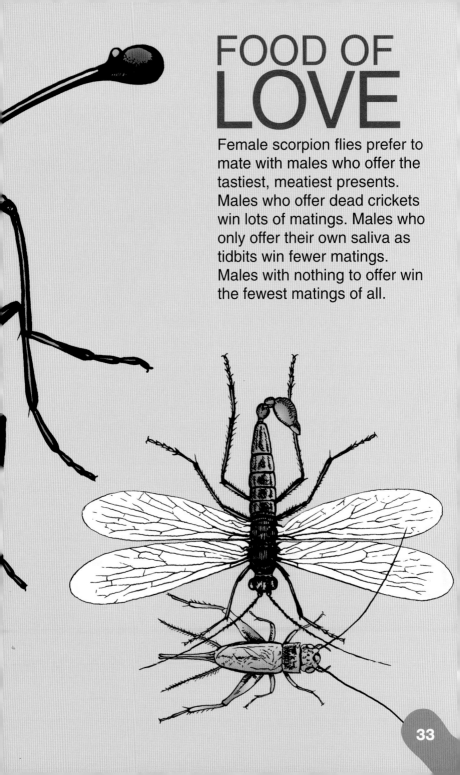

AWHALE
OF A TIME 1

Most whales have complicated courtships involving lots of caressing, nuzzling and rubbing before mating. Among humpback whales, courtship involves large groups racing along the surface and leaping clear of the water, landing on their backs with huge splashes. They then mate face to face in a vertical position with their heads out of the water.

KISS OF **DEATH**

The male cuttlefish prepares for mating by displaying and using all his colors to attract a female. The pair mate head to head with their tentacles locked together and the male places a sperm packet in the female's mantle. After mating the male dies. The female lays her eggs and then she also dies. The parents never see their children and all the baby cuttlefish are born orphans.

PAPA'S POUCH PREGNANCY

Among seahorses the role of the sexes is reversed. During mating the female introduces her eggs into a special pouch on the male's abdomen with an organ resembling a penis. The male fertilizes the eggs inside his body, and carries them in his pouch until they hatch out and develop to maturity. During this time the pouch swells enormously, and he is visibly pregnant. Finally, the young are ready to be "born," and the male appears to suffer birth pangs.

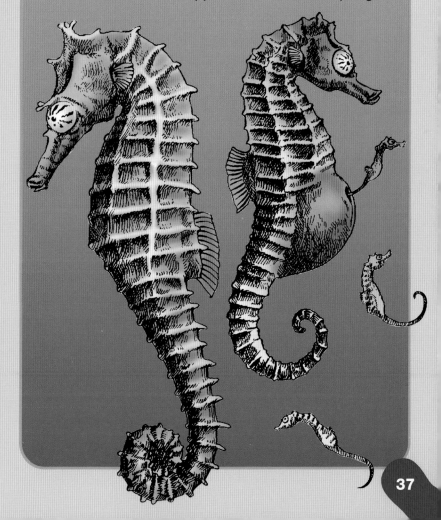

KISSING**FISH**

Two kissing gouramis sometimes stay stuck mouth to mouth for nearly half an hour. This is no kiss between a loving couple, though. It is a fight for territory between two rival males. Tiny teeth in their lips help lock their mouths together for a trial of strength.

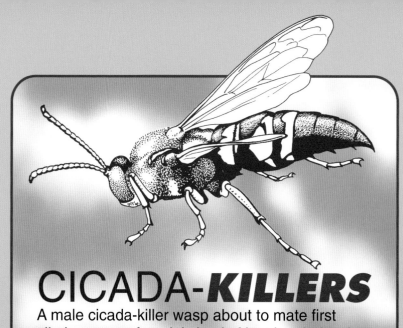

CICADA-**KILLERS**

A male cicada-killer wasp about to mate first climbs upon a female's back. Next he shakes her head with his front legs. Then he taps her feelers with his own, rubbing on a sex scent that puts her in the mood. After a few seconds mating on her back he dismounts and they stay stuck together tail to tail for more than half an hour.

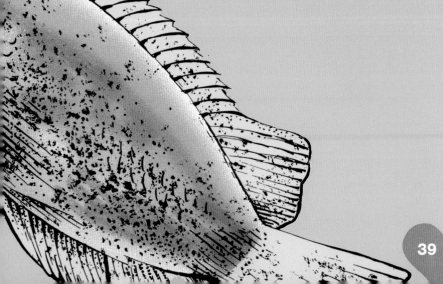

WATER SPORTS

A pair of Ganges River dolphins take part in a courtship ritual that includes chasing each other and leaping out of the water together. When it is time to mate they hold on to each other with their flippers and engage in belly contact, sometimes while upright. Young are born within eight to nine months.

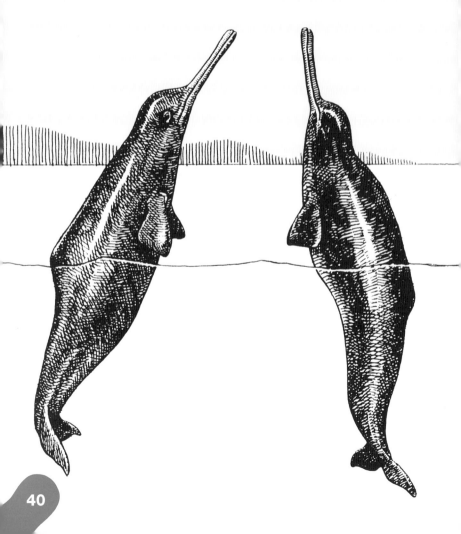

A WHALE
OF A TIME 2

The gray whales' courting ritual involves two males and one female. Only one male mates and the pair stay joined for about an hour with the female on top. During this time the second male never leaves them, mostly lying back to back with the female, or staying at her side. Over a year later a calf is born and within thirty minutes the baby whale can swim.

SHAKE YOUR
TAIL FEATHERS

In the mating ritual of the peafowl the peacock uses his brilliant tail display to attract a peahen, who is smaller and plainly colored. He puffs out his chest and struts by the nearest female, shaking and rattling his magnificent feathers as he goes. If the hen is attracted she will run around to face him again so that he can continue his display. This ritual will be repeated a number of times until the female invites the peacock to mate by crouching in front of him.

MATING MERMAIDS

Mating sea cows are a mass of threshing flippers. In shallow water 20 male manatees may jostle one another as they chase one female. Shoving and chasing lasts up to three weeks, while the female is in estrous. At last one male succeeds, and mates belly to belly, with the female on top. She may mate with more males after that.

SPAWNING
STARFISH

Most male or female starfish send eggs
or sperm from sex organs in their arms to
the center of the body then out into the
sea. The six-armed sea star female,
though, retains her eggs. Once these are
fertilized her tiny tube feet transfer them
below her body. There, beneath arched
arms, she keeps them clean and broods
her eggs and young.

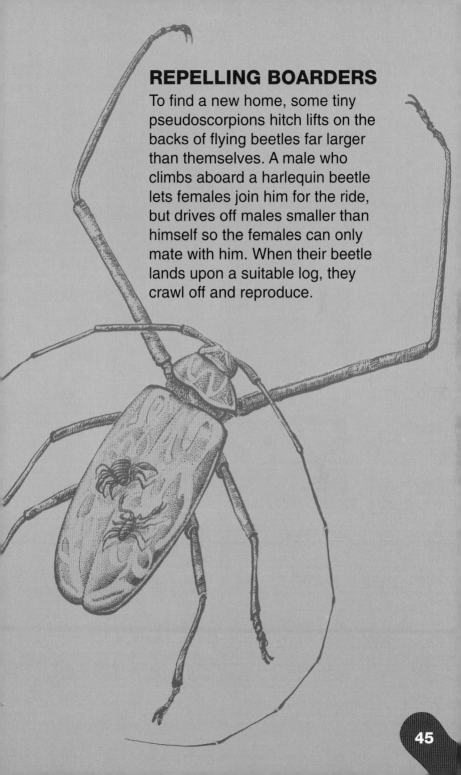

REPELLING BOARDERS

To find a new home, some tiny pseudoscorpions hitch lifts on the backs of flying beetles far larger than themselves. A male who climbs aboard a harlequin beetle lets females join him for the ride, but drives off males smaller than himself so the females can only mate with him. When their beetle lands upon a suitable log, they crawl off and reproduce.

BOUNCING BIRDS

Two long-tailed manakin males woo a female with a song and leapfrog dance. Both then bounce up and down upon a twig. After that the junior male flies away while the senior male flutters out and back. If a watching female likes this show she joins him on the twig and there the couple mate. Meanwhile Junior gains nothing but experience.

A **CRABBY** COUPLE

A male blue crab waves claws and kicks up sand to woo a female, then carries her about for days tucked in beneath his legs. He stands guard when she molts, then turns her upside down, and grasps her so their bellies touch. Now his "sex legs" transfer sperm into two openings beneath her body. There they fertilize all the eggs that she will lay throughout her life.

LEKKING

Each spring up to 30 male sage grouse will display to females at a dancing ground, or lek. Each male takes strutting steps, lifts and drops his wings, blows up big yellow air sacs on his neck, then lets the air out with a wheezing pop. Only a few males get to mate with all the females attracted to this show.

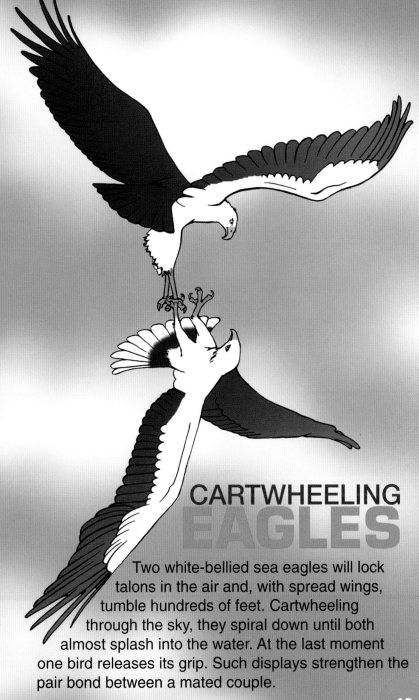

CARTWHEELING
EAGLES

Two white-bellied sea eagles will lock talons in the air and, with spread wings, tumble hundreds of feet. Cartwheeling through the sky, they spiral down until both almost splash into the water. At the last moment one bird releases its grip. Such displays strengthen the pair bond between a mated couple.

LOVE DUST

A male silver-washed fritillary seduces a female by showering her with "love dust." As he flutters near her, special capsules in his forewings burst open at weak points to release a cloud of scent she cannot resist. His scent capsules are special versions of the overlapping scales that cover every butterfly's wings.

SELFSTARTER

The mangrove fish is the only backboned animal to fertilize itself. This little Caribbean species produces eggs and sperm in organs known as ovotestes. The sperm fertilize the eggs while these are still inside the fish's body. Mangrove fish share land crabs' burrows, and even wriggle overland to reach them.

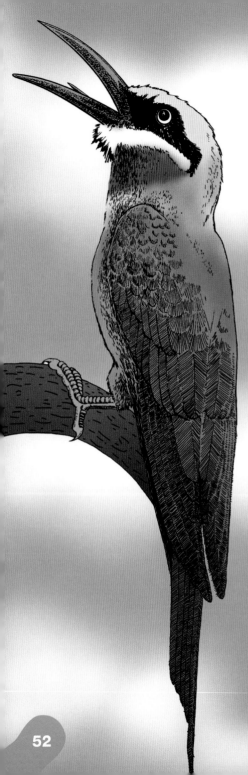

BIRD *CHASE*

White-fronted bee-eaters form enduring pairs, yet females are often subject to male sexual aggression. When a female leaves her nest hole, up to 12 males may chase her, try to pin her to the ground, and then compete to mate. Surprisingly, these pursuers are not single males but males who already have mates of their own.

FLY
FIGHTS

Seaweed flies engage in furious struggles to decide which individuals are fit to mate. In one species a female acts like a bucking bronco, kicking and shaking in her efforts to dislodge the male from her back, and curving her body down away from his. A large, fit male comes out successful from this test. When such a couple mates, its offspring are likely to be fit and strong.

PAPER, SCISSORS, STONE

Male side-blotched lizards' sexual strategies are like paper-scissors-stone, a game of strengths and weaknesses. Big, aggressive, orange-throated males control large areas and many females. Smaller, less aggressive, blue-throated males control small areas with maybe just one female each. Resembling females, yellow-throated males control no partners but mate sneakily with those of other males.

PENIS FENCING

When two flatworms of one oceanic species meet, a sex fight invariably follows. Though both are male and female, each tries to pierce the other with its penis, pointed like a hypodermic syringe. As one lunges the other dodges and strikes back. This fight can last an hour before one duelist makes a hit, injecting sperm into the other—anywhere will do. The winner then swims off.

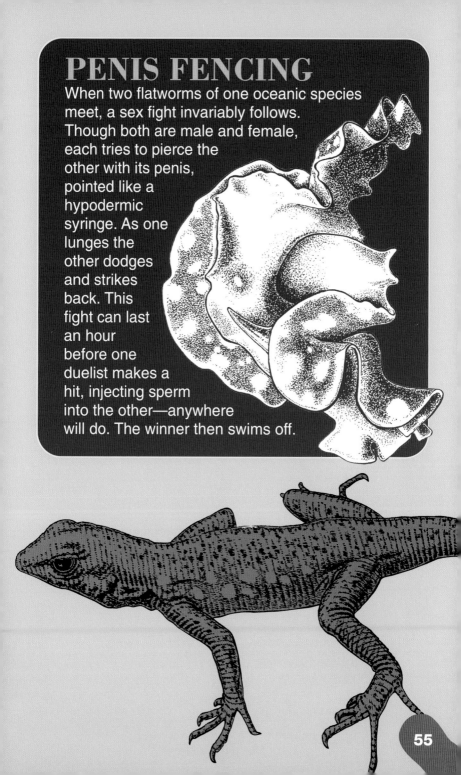

BIG AND BUTCH

Males who fight other males to win a group of females must be big and strong—much bigger and much stronger than the females. A male southern elephant seal can be ten times heavier and twice the length of the females that he mates with.

FIGHTING **FROGS**

Gladiator frogs get their name from the
vicious way males fight each other over
females. These tropical tree frogs lash out
with switchblade "knives"—sharp,
retractable spines, one on each hand just
above the thumb. Aiming at an enemy's
eyes and eardrums, they often badly hurt
and sometimes kill each other. With life so
brutal, it is usually short. Most males are
dead within a year.

SPIDER**SEX**

A male spider maneuvers sperm produced beneath his body onto leglike head appendages called pedipalps. To fertilize a female's eggs he must poke at least one pedipalp into the vagina beneath her body. A female tarantula rears to help the male, while both stand face to face.

SHOWY **SHOULDERS**

Bats hang upside down to mate, the female embraced by the male's wings from behind. First, though, the female must be wooed. To attract the females flying past their branches, groups of male epauletted bats flaunt long white tufts of shoulder hair. They also puff out their cheeks, call out, and beat their wings to waft their scent toward the females.

SEX LEGS

A many-legged male millipede curls up to transfer sperm created in his body's second segment to his seventh segment's gonopods or "sex legs." He then courts a female by walking on her back. If she lifts her front end, the couple intertwine. His sex legs now pass her a sperm packet to fertilize the eggs that she will later lay in a hole dug in the ground.

DYING
FOR LOVE

When a male honeybee, a drone, mates with a queen, his sex organs break off inside her with a loud pop. The drone bleeds to death but his sex organs stay inside to fertilize her eggs. By plugging her sex opening they may help to keep out rival males.

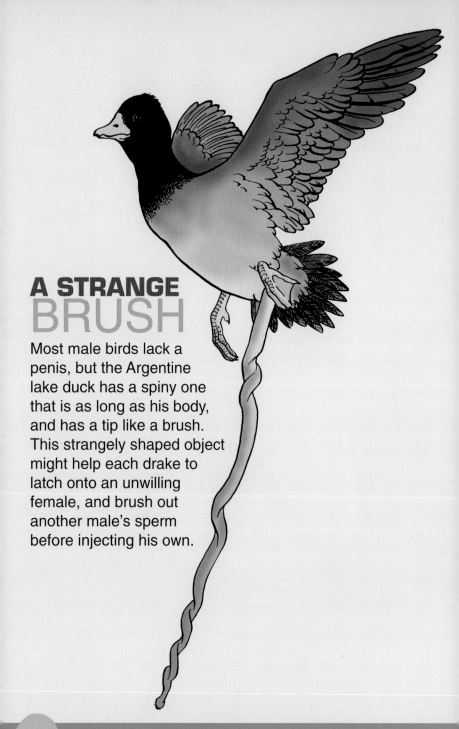

A STRANGE
BRUSH

Most male birds lack a penis, but the Argentine lake duck has a spiny one that is as long as his body, and has a tip like a brush. This strangely shaped object might help each drake to latch onto an unwilling female, and brush out another male's sperm before injecting his own.

MAKING SURE

If a male hedge sparrow suspects another male has mated with his partner, he pecks her cloaca, which then lets out a droplet containing sperm. This way he helps to make sure no other male will fertilize her eggs and that only he will be the father of the couple's baby birds.

ALL AT SEA

Male jellyfish fertilize females' eggs while drifting in the sea. Their larvae settle on the seabed and grow into plantlike polyps. From each polyp more bud off. Then the first forms a pile of tiny "saucers" that pinch off one by one and swim away, becoming adult jellyfish.

BREED FAST, DIE YOUNG

Little *Nothobranchius* fish may start spawning just three weeks after they hatch. They have to breed quickly for the shallow pools where they live will dry up. All the fish then die. Their eggs, though, survive in the mud, and hatch when the next rainy season refills their pools.

SEE YOU LATER
ALLIGATOR

Courting alligators nudge and rub against each other. They grunt, bellow, blow bubbles, and try to push each other underwater. The male then mounts the female so that their cloacas meet. As with other reptiles, each sex has this type of opening that also lets out body waste. But a penis pops out from the male's cloaca, injecting sperm into the female's oviduct.

STACKING UP

Slipper limpets form stacks of up to 15 mating males and females. Males mate with the females below them, but themselves turn into females as they grow. The top male's penis is so long that he can often manage mating with the female at the bottom of the pile.

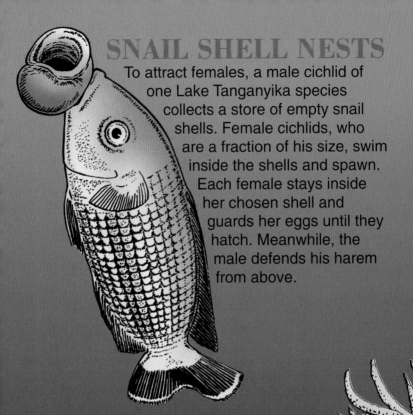

SNAIL SHELL NESTS

To attract females, a male cichlid of one Lake Tanganyika species collects a store of empty snail shells. Female cichlids, who are a fraction of his size, swim inside the shells and spawn. Each female stays inside her chosen shell and guards her eggs until they hatch. Meanwhile, the male defends his harem from above.

SYNCHRONIZED
SPAWNING

Coral polyps live fixed in stony cups on coral reefs, so cannot meet to mate. But on a few moonlit nights each year millions of the polyps shed trillions of sex cells in the sea. There, sperm meet eggs, producing swimming young. These drift with ocean currents then settle down as cup-building coral polyps on the seabed.

MIGHTY MOLAS

A female ocean sunfish can contain 300 million eggs in her ovaries, a record for any backboned animal. No other shows as great a size difference between a mother and her fry (hatchlings). Fry 0.01 inches (1.27 mm) long can grow to weigh 2 tons. In fact this species, *Mola mola*, is the heaviest bony fish there is.

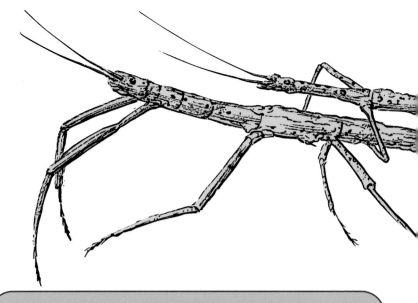

LIVING VESUVIUS

Giant clams produce more eggs than any other animal. Resembling an undersea volcano, a giant clam may squirt a billion eggs and billions of sperm into the surrounding sea. What is more, the clam repeats this every year for 30 years or more. Few eggs meet sperm this way, so reproduction depends on mass production.

MATING **MARATHON**

Few animals make love longer than a certain kind of stick insect. A male climbs aboard a female twice his size and stays there for up to ten weeks. The couple mate all through that time. If he dismounted any sooner, another male might take his place. His mating marathon ensures that he alone will fertilize her eggs.

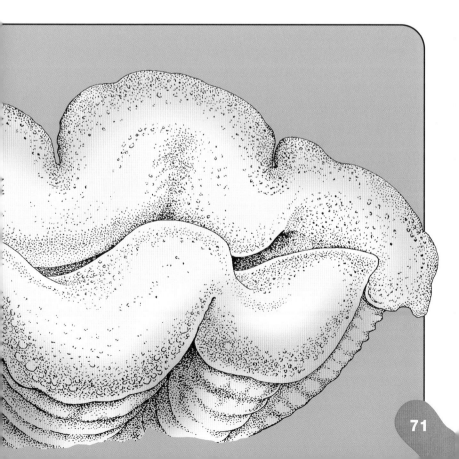

CLOACAL KISS

Most male birds lack a penis. Each sex releases body
waste and sperm or eggs through a hole called a cloaca.
When pigeons mate the female turns her tail aside so that
the swollen lips of their cloacas meet. In the few moments
of this brief "cloacal kiss" sperm swim into the female's
oviduct, perhaps to wait for weeks to fertilize the eggs
maturing in her ovary.

TINY TESTES

A male gorilla has tinier testicles than a chimpanzee one-fifth his weight. Small sperm factories are big enough for the gorilla, for he alone will mate with all the females in his group. But a female chimpanzee may mate with several males, so each must make sperm in abundance to stand a chance of fathering her young.

STUCK TOGETHER

After a dog has mated with a bitch, the two stay stuck together for up to an hour. For all that time his penis is so swollen in her body that he cannot pull it out. Because his penis plugs her birth canal his sperm cannot leak out and no other dog can fertilize her eggs to become the father of her pups.

LOVE
BITES

Sharks mate face to face
with help from two grooved,
stiffened fins called claspers
underneath the belly of the male.
Sperm packets shot out from the male's body
pass through a clasper and on into the
female's reproductive tract. Meanwhile her
fearsome lover may deliver bites that leave
her body scarred. No wonder some female
sharks need thick skin for protection.

OUCH!

So that their sex organs met, even the heaviest male dinosaurs must have leaned on the females' backs. Now and then a giant dinosaur's weight quite likely injured the female. Rough courtship may explain why some duckbilled dinosaurs had crumpled bones at the root of the tail.

DESIRABLE DROPPINGS

Female red-backed salamanders sniff the droppings left
by males outside their holes. This tells them if the
males have been eating termites or ants. Termites are
thinner-skinned, juicier, and more nourishing than ants,
so termite-eating males are likely to be fit and strong.
Female salamanders prefer to mate with these males.

A SAFER
FOSTER HOME

A female bitterling lays eggs inside a mussel. She injects them through her long egg-laying tube, which she pokes inside the mussel's shell. A male bitterling then sheds sperm in the water above. When the mussel breathes in, sperm sucked in with water fertilizes the eggs. Later, baby fish will swim out through the mussel's breathing tube.

DANCING *SCORPIONS*

Male and female scorpions "dance" face to face with interlocking claws. The male lays a sperm packet on the ground, then drags the female over it. She draws the packet up into an opening in her belly so the sperm will fertilize her eggs. Months later these will have developed into babies that pop out, crawl up her legs, and ride upon her back.

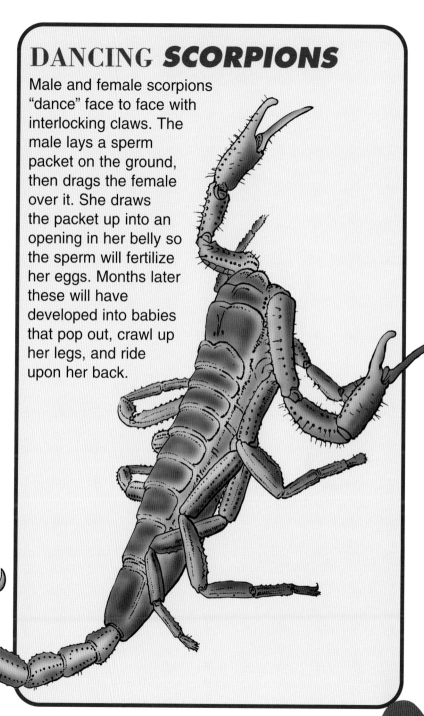

TAKING OVER

If two spreading colonies of star-shaped sea squirts meet and join upon the ocean floor, one may send cells to the other through the blood supply they come to share. Genes from the stronger colony then find their way into the other's sperm and eggs. This way the dominant colony becomes part-parent of the other's offspring.

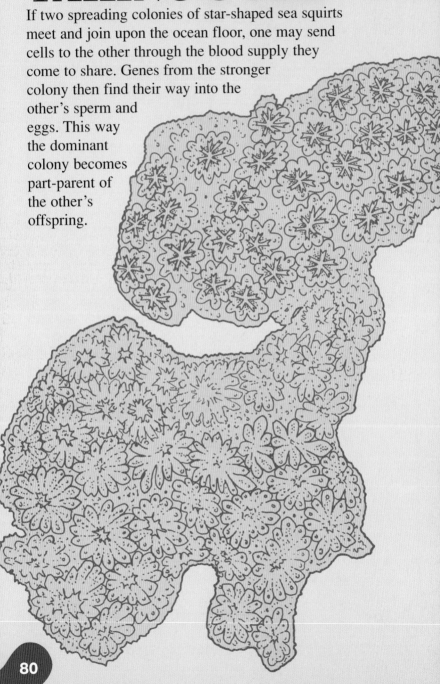

LOVE *RATS*

In six hours one male brown rat may mate with up to 20 females. In one year a pair of brown rats could produce 15,000 descendants. In fact this never happens. Accidents, disease, hunger, and predators including people kill off most of the couple's children and their offspring.

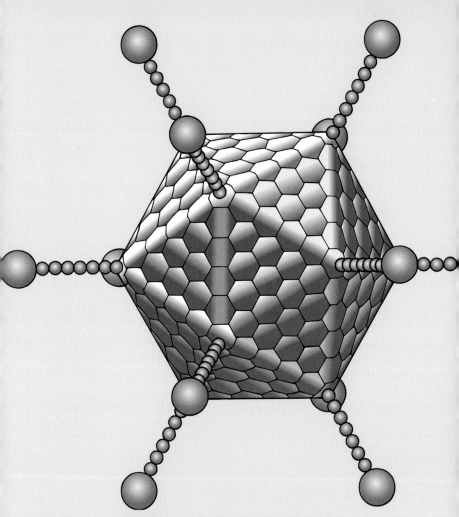

BACTERIA-*EATERS*

Bacteriophages are not animals but microscopic viruses that breed at the expense of bacteria larger than themselves. A T4 bacteriophage resembles a spaceship's six-legged landing pod. Settling on a bacterium of a kind found in your gut, the T4 injects it with DNA that turns the bacterium's contents into new T4s. The bacterium bursts open and the T4s all escape.

LOVENEST

The male bower bird spends months building a bower, which he decorates with pretty stones, berries, moss, and bright objects. When a female visits the glittering nest he performs a dance and the pair mate. The female then leaves and builds a very simple nest in which to lay her eggs.

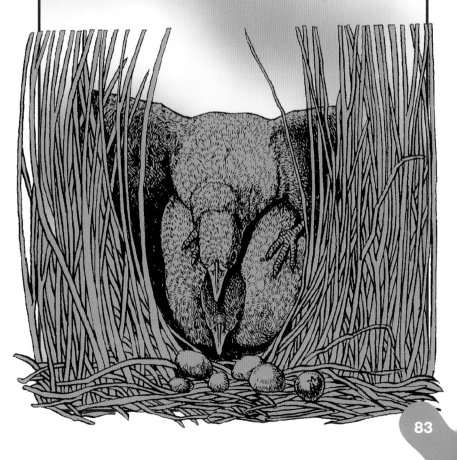

EGGS ON TOADS

Surinam toads mate in the water, and when the female releases her eggs the male fertilizes them and then presses them onto her back. Here a skin grows enclosing the eggs in their own little cells. Eighty days later the eggs hatch and young toads emerge.

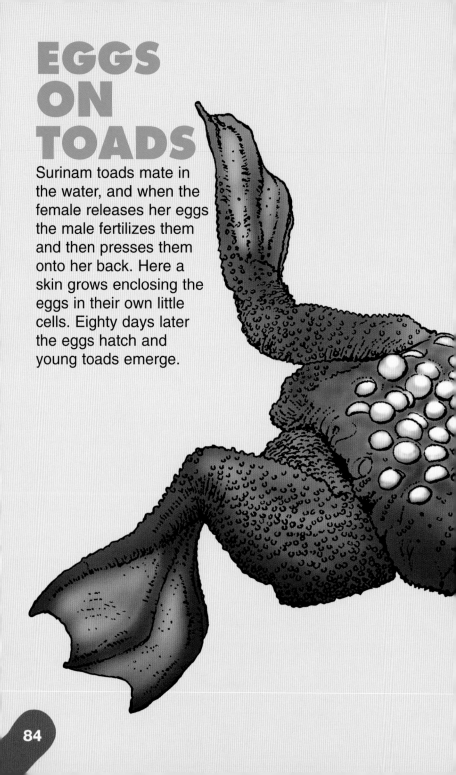

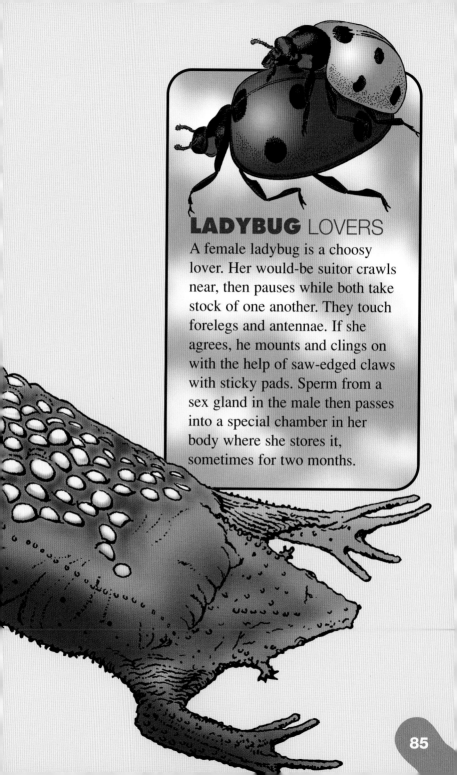

LADYBUG LOVERS

A female ladybug is a choosy lover. Her would-be suitor crawls near, then pauses while both take stock of one another. They touch forelegs and antennae. If she agrees, he mounts and clings on with the help of saw-edged claws with sticky pads. Sperm from a sex gland in the male then passes into a special chamber in her body where she stores it, sometimes for two months.

BONY STIFFENERS

In cats, dogs, and many other mammals, males have a penis-stiffening bone called the *os pubis*. In the walrus this bony support is nearly as long as a man's arm.

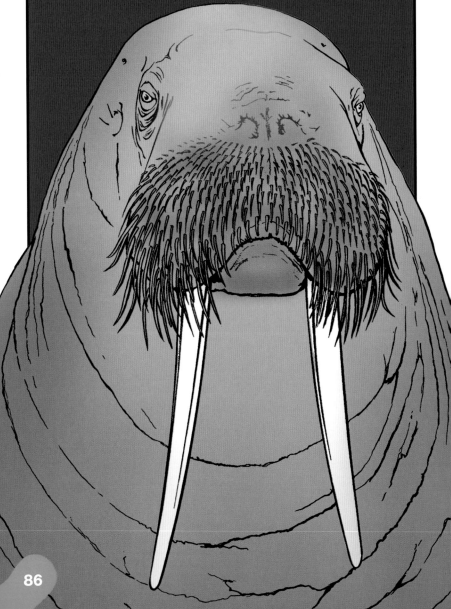

CAN YOU DIG IT?

The biggest nests of any bird are built by the mallee bird, which amazingly builds its own compost heap to incubate its eggs. After digging a hole up to 15 feet (4.6 m) wide and 3 feet (0.9 m) deep they fill it with vegetation. The eggs are laid into this and, as the vegetation rots, they heat up. The birds then cover the mound with sand to keep the correct temperature. When the young hatch they have to burrow their own way out of a mound that can weigh up to 300 tons.

JUST **GIRLS**

In most backboned animals only eggs fertilized by males produce young. But some kinds of whiptail lizards are all female. Two females will pair up like a male and female. Then one lays unfertilized eggs that hatch into more females.

NO

E(GG)XAG-GERATION

The chicken-sized kiwi lays an egg more than ten times the size of a chicken's egg, and nearly one-quarter the weight of its mother. No other bird lays an egg so large compared to its own size. Sometimes an egg is too large to pop out and the unfortunate mother dies with the egg still stuck inside her.

BORN IN A
FOAM NEST

Frog spawn laid in water can be
eaten by fish. Some frogs prevent
this by mating and laying eggs on a
leaf overhanging a stream. Each
female frog beats sticky mucus into a
foam nest that keeps her eggs moist.
When they hatch, tadpoles slither
down from the nest, drop into the
water, and swim off.

CANNIBAL DAD

A Japanese cardinal fish swims around with a mouthful of babies. This way he protects his young until they are big enough to swim away safely on their own. But if he spots a more attractive female than their mother he swallows his children and woos the new female instead.

MALE MIDWIVES

Bell-like calls draw female midwife toads to males' burrows. Grasping a female round the waist, a male massages her sex opening with his toes until she lays a string of eggs. After fertilizing these he wraps them around his hind limbs and walks away. Weeks later he takes a dip in a pond. Tadpoles now break free from the eggs and swim off.

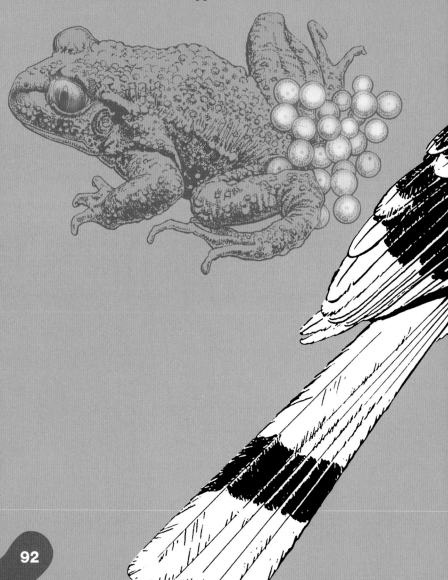

BORN
IN JAIL

The great hornbill nests inside a hollow tree, plastering the entrance hole with droppings, wood, and food scraps. Just a slit remains to poke her beak through when her mate brings food. For months the female's eggs and chicks stay safe inside this prison until her young are strong enough to fly away.

MS. INTO MR.

Some kinds of wrasse or "cleaner fish" can switch sex from female to male. In one tropical reef species, an aggressive male lives and breeds with three to six females. If he dies, the oldest female turns male and takes his place.

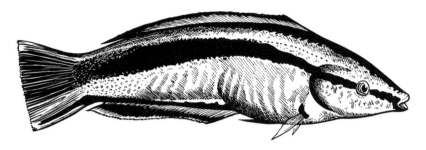

HAREM HUSBANDS

Bronze-winged jacanas are long-toed tropical waterbirds whose females leave child-rearing to the males. One female mates with up to four males in the territory she controls. The males do everything else: They build nests, incubate the eggs the female lays, and feed the chicks that hatch. This way a jacana with four husbands produces four times more babies than a female with just one.

MIXED UP

Whooper cranes reared by people risk growing up to think themselves human and to seek humans as mates. To ensure that these rare birds grow up to mate with each other, hand-rearers wear whooper crane puppet disguises.

DADDY DEAREST

The male stickleback takes the lead in caring for his young. He builds a nest and to attract a female performs a zig-zag dance and shows a special orange color. The female enters the nest and the male encourages her to lay her eggs. The male then fertilizes the eggs and he alone stays near the nest to protect the eggs. After they are hatched he continues looking after the young until they can lead independent lives.

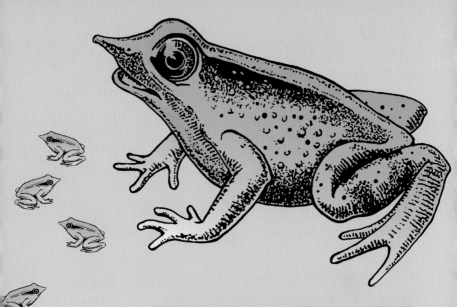

SWALLOWED
ALIVE

A female Darwin's frog lays eggs on moist ground. Male frogs fertilize the eggs, guard them until they hatch, then pop them into their mouths. Inside each male's vocal sac, nourishing tissue helps the tadpoles develop into froglets. The male then opens his mouth and out they jump.

LOVE DART

The "parasitic worm" discovered in a female paper nautilus, a relative of the octopus, turns out to be the penis of a male, a fraction of the female's size. Developed rolled up in a cyst, each male's third, sperm-bearing arm breaks off inside a female, where it stays for some time, looking alive and wormlike.

QUEEN RAT

Naked mole-rats are the mammal equivalent of ants. Like an ant nest, an underground mole-rat colony has workers, soldiers, and a queen, the only breeding female. She stays that way because her daughters smear themselves with her urine containing a substance that prevents them from becoming sexually active.

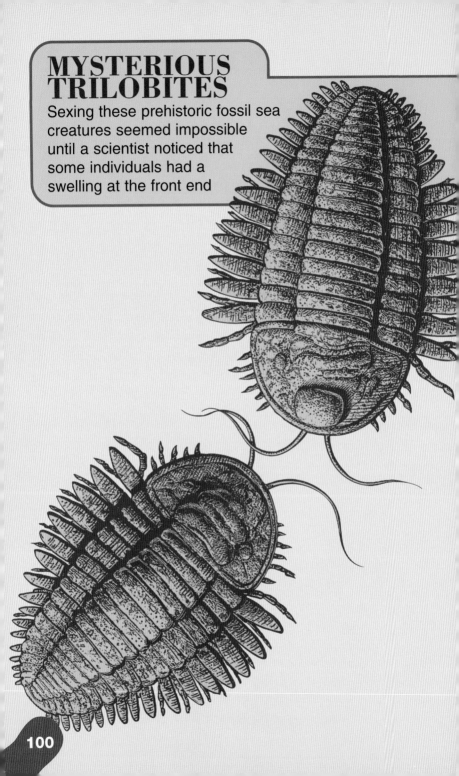

MYSTERIOUS TRILOBITES

Sexing these prehistoric fossil sea creatures seemed impossible until a scientist noticed that some individuals had a swelling at the front end of the head, while other individuals had none. Most likely the swelling was a brood pouch where young trilobites had developed safe from predators. Adults with a brood pouch would have been the females, and those without, the males.

LONGEST
PREGNANCY

A mated female elephant goes 20 months before giving birth. That is more than two and a half times the length of an average human pregnancy, and the longest gestation period for any mammal. There are even records of baby elephants born after a gestation lasting more than two years.

TEEMING TENRECS

Among the most prolific mammals are Madagascar's tenrecs: small, slim-snouted creatures, some resembling hedgehogs. A female streaked tenrec can breed at only three weeks old, and a female tailless tenrec once gave birth to 32 babies. This was the largest litter known to have been produced by any wild mammal, though not all her family survived.

TREKKING TOTS

A kangaroo is born blind, naked, no longer than a human thumb joint, and as light as a nickel. Yet this scrap of life at once squirms through its mother's fur and fastens itself onto a nipple in her belly pouch. There it feeds and grows for more than seven months. When big enough it leaves, but it can hop back in if danger threatens.

INCESTUOUS **MITES**

A female of one kind of microscopic mite grows fat by guzzling a thrip's egg. Meanwhile her own eggs hatch inside her to produce a male and up to eight female mites. The male mates with his sisters. They all then gobble up their mother. She dies, bursts open, and her pregnant daughters escape.

SHORTEST
PREGNANCY

A female Virginia opossum can give birth only 11 days after mating. That is the shortest pregnancy for any North American mammal, and among the shortest in the world. As with all marsupials, her babies emerge tiny and underdeveloped. They spend 10 weeks completing their development inside her belly pouch.

COOL GIRLS

A hatchling turtle's sex depends on how warm it was while still inside its egg. A snapping turtle's eggs incubated in warm sand all hatch out as boys. But snapping turtle eggs that are laid in cool or hot sand all hatch out as girls.

WHO IS DAD?

A female chimpanzee can have sex with eight males in 15 minutes. Perhaps she does so as insurance. If some males are more fertile than others it would

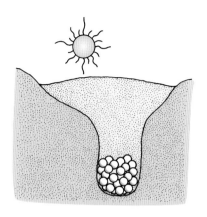

help to make sure she gets pregnant. Or it might protect her future child. A jealous male will kill another's offspring, but every male who has mated with a female might suppose he is her baby's father.

GOING *CRAZY*

Some males go to bizarre lengths to impress a would-be mate. Perched on a branch, a male blue bird of paradise swings backward and hangs upside down. In that absurd position he spreads the brilliantly colored feathers of his breast to form a fan that swells and shrinks in time to a noise like a mechanical drill—his courtship song.

SURFING TO SPAWN

On certain nights of the year small silvery fish called grunion ride big waves far up Californian shores. Each male wraps himself around a female, fertilizing her eggs as she drills tail-first into wet sand to spawn. Moments later waves carry them both back to sea. After two weeks or so another high tide will rescue their hatchlings.

A CAUTIOUS COURTSHIP

A courting male orb-web spider risks being eaten by the much larger female. Waiting in the middle of her web she pounces on any creature entangled in its strands. He therefore strums upon them in a special way to signal his approach. Then he creeps toward her, paying out a silken safety rope. If she mistakes him for a meal this will swiftly carry him to safety.

TREACHERY

Male common fireflies home in on the flashing lights given off by the flirtatious females of their own species. But a hungry female woods firefly can copy these signals to lure one of these males to his doom. He lands by her side expecting some fun with a mate, only to find that she eats him instead.

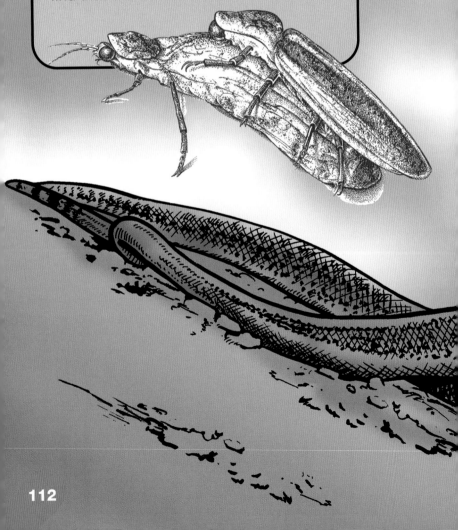

TWO PENISES

Male snakes have hemipenes—a pair of penises—
below the base of the tail. When a male mates
with a female, one enters her cloaca and delivers
sperm. Spines sticking out around
the swollen penis improve its
grip and stop it slipping
out too soon.

MISMATCHED

Besides mating with female dolphins, male dolphins sometimes try making love to extremely unsuitable partners. People have seen bottlenose dolphins try to have sex with anything from turtles and sharks to eels and women.

KING OF THE CASTLE

A male topi (African antelope) stands on an old termite mound waiting hopefully for females to mate with. Dozens more males guard their own little patches of ground all around. Females weave their way through these courts to mate with the strongest male, the one who holds court in the middle.

KEEPING HIM
FAITHFUL

If a male starling woos other females, his mate will offer him sex. She will also discourage her rivals by chasing them off and planting "occupied" signs (nesting material) in any available nest holes. A possessive female can annoy her mate so much that he drives her back to the family nest.

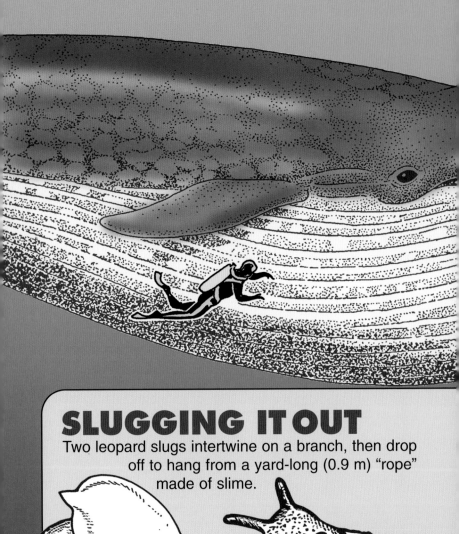

SLUGGING IT OUT

Two leopard slugs intertwine on a branch, then drop
off to hang from a yard-long (0.9 m) "rope"
made of slime.

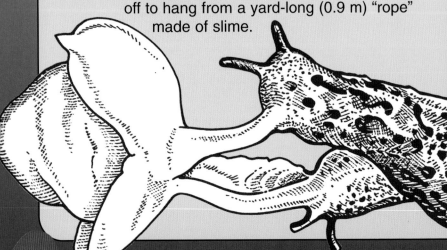

WHAT A **DORK!**

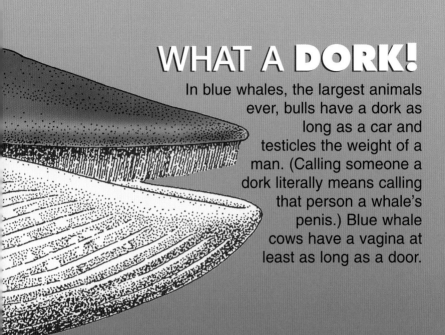

In blue whales, the largest animals ever, bulls have a dork as long as a car and testicles the weight of a man. (Calling someone a dork literally means calling that person a whale's penis.) Blue whale cows have a vagina at least as long as a door.

From each creature's head now sprouts a dangling penis. Both penis tips meet and swap sperm. Slugs are hermaphrodites (each is both male and female), but they fertilize each other's eggs.

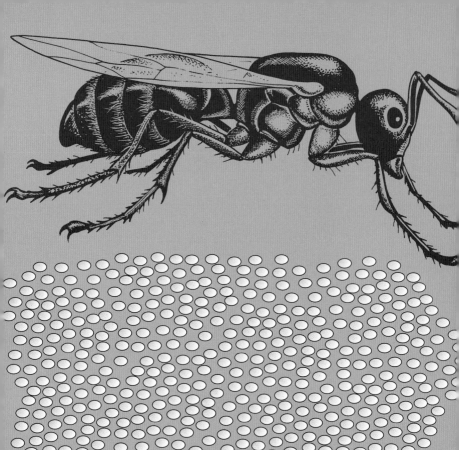

SPERM **BANK**

On her nuptial flight, a queen ant meets with one or two males, who inject her with sperm. She banks this in her body. Her brief sexual encounters supply enough sperm to fertilize all the eggs she will lay throughout the rest of her life—many thousands of eggs in a lifetime that could last 15 years.

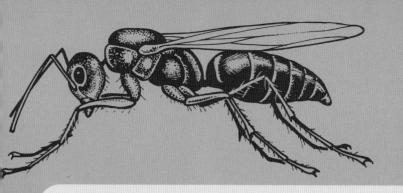

BUBBLE NESTERS

Bettas (fighting fish) mate below a nest of floating bubbles. The male who blew them spreads his fins to show off to a female, then wraps himself around her to fertilize the eggs she lays. The eggs sink but he pops them in his mouth and blows them up beneath the bubble nest. There he guards them until the babies hatch and swim about.

SCENTED EMPRESS

A female emperor moth sits on a low bush, wafting scent from a gland in her abdomen. If even a few of her airborne scent particles reach a male's feathery antennae, he will follow the scent trail upwind to its source. Males are said to be able to track down a female as much as 3 miles (5 km) away.

GRASPING
SHRIMPS

A mating male brine shrimp grips a female
with antennae that have evolved into
"graspers." The tiny eggs that she
lays will float on the salty lake
where they live. If this
completely dries up, her
eggs will survive for years
in the dusty ground,
hatching when rainwater
refills the lake.

CORKSCREWING

A boar's penis has a corkscrew-shaped tip. A sow has a corkscrew-shaped cervix. When a boar mounts a sow and starts thrusting, his penis screws itself into her cervix. Once his penis achieves a tight fit he ejaculates sperm. Conceivably, cross-threading could cause an uncomfortable problem.

LOVE SONG

Each spring male sedge warblers attract females by singing long and loudly. The best songsters are the first to win mates. But a female won by a fine serenade is in for an unwelcome surprise: once he has wooed and won her, her partner shuts up.

TOOTHY
TRAP

When sagebrush crickets mate the female enjoys chewing the male's stubby little wings. Meanwhile, a toothy trap on the male's back grips her belly. This stops her from escaping if she finds his wings already chewed by another female.

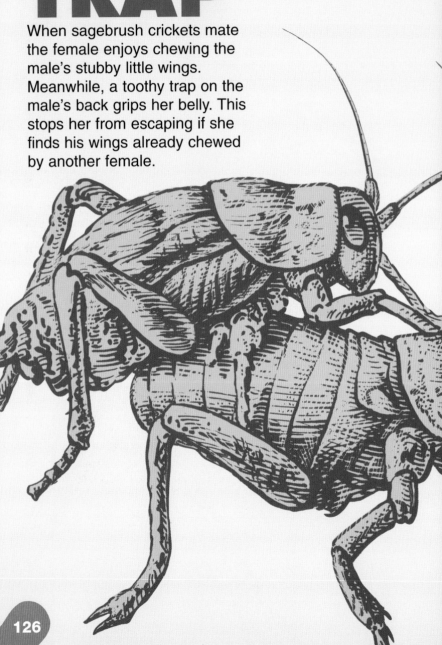

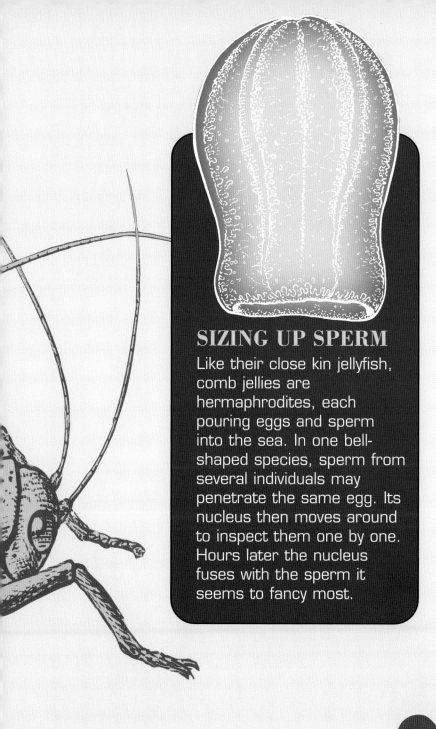

SIZING UP SPERM

Like their close kin jellyfish, comb jellies are hermaphrodites, each pouring eggs and sperm into the sea. In one bell-shaped species, sperm from several individuals may penetrate the same egg. Its nucleus then moves around to inspect them one by one. Hours later the nucleus fuses with the sperm it seems to fancy most.

INFANTICIDE

Sometimes a new male lion drives off the lion who had fathered the cubs of a pride. The newcomer ruthlessly murders the youngest of these cubs and then mates with their mothers. In this cruel way the new male stamps his genetic influence on the group.

TEAMWORK

In Florida, scrub jays work as a family team to raise young. Instead of rearing their own families, the previous year's young help their mother and father feed and protect the parents' next brood. Helping their brothers and sisters improves their chance of survival in a land that lacks plenty of food.

MATING **VOLCANOES**

Resembling mini volcanoes, barnacles live fixed to seashore rocks yet they can meet to mate. Each unrolls a long, narrow, tube-shaped penis. This pokes out from the creature's shell and slides inside a neighbor's to fertilize its eggs. The neighbor may do likewise in return, for each barnacle has male and female organs.

PARTNERS
FOR LIFE

Few birds mate for life but albatrosses do. The world's longest courtship cements the bond between them. Royal albatrosses clap beaks, rub them together, moo, point beaks toward the sky, and dance around each other with spread wings. They may repeat this ritual for three annual breeding seasons before they actually mate.

A WIGGLY COCOON

Earthworms have both male and female organs. When they mate they are stuck together at the "saddle" in the middle of their bodies and sperm is exchanged and stored in a receptacle. Once its eggs are ready each worm pushes the saddle up its body to where the eggs are, then continues to push it further until it is completely separated from the worm's body and becomes a cocoon. Only now can the eggs be fertilized.

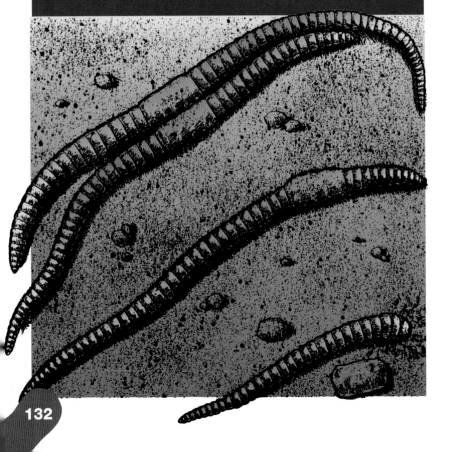

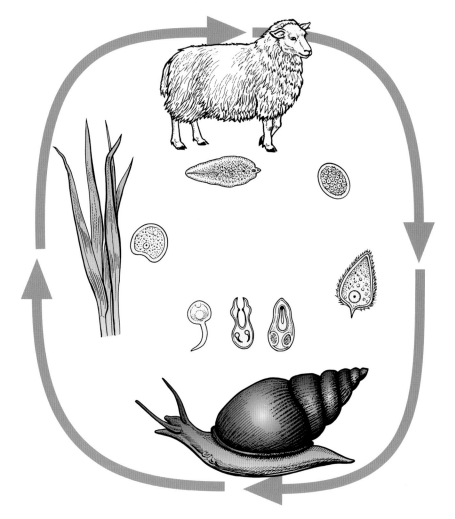

A LIFE CYCLE

Parasitic worms called liver flukes lead complex
reproductive lives. Two lay eggs and swap sperm inside
the bile duct of a sheep. These eggs end up in the
sheep's feces where they hatch into larvae that form
cysts in water snails. Each unfertilized cyst produces
fresh individuals. These and their offspring similarly
multiply. The offspring then form cysts. From encysted
offspring swallowed by a sheep young flukes emerge
and grow inside its liver.

BIRDBALLET

Mass courtship is the rule among lesser flamingos. Hundreds of birds with necks erect and heads held high form a phalanx that struts through a shallow lake. Here and there birds flap their wings, showing splashes of color, and rival males peck one another. Then partnerships form and pairs nest on mud mounds in the water.

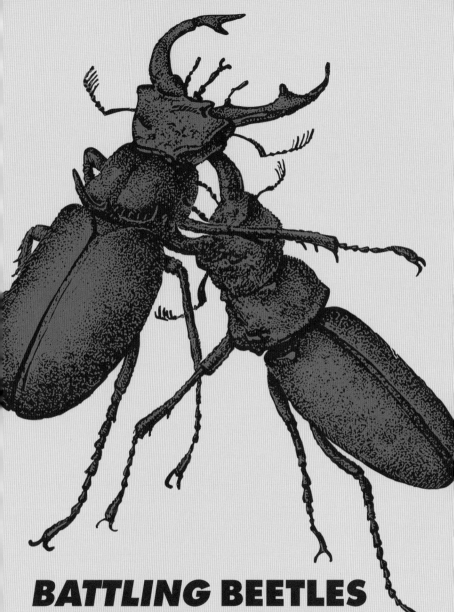

BATTLING **BEETLES**

At mating time, male stag beetles joust like rival stags. If one strays onto another's rotting log they grapple, rearing until one tumbles over. With his antlerlike mandibles, the other grasps him round the middle, lifts him in the air, then hurls him to the ground. The loser usually scuttles off unharmed.

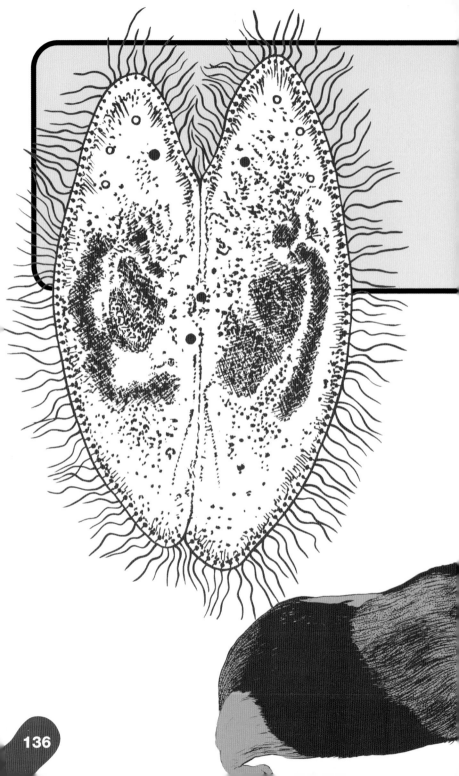

TWO MAKE TWO

Slipper-shaped *Paramecium* is a microscopic organism that usually reproduces by splitting into two. Sometimes, though, two individuals from different strains fuse to remake themselves. Swapping genetic material, they become identical twins. These then separate and each splits to breed in the usual way. If a *Paramecium's* offspring all survived, in 113 days their volume would equal the Earth's.

LOCKED OUT

When two guinea pigs mate, some of the male's sperm and seminal fluid forms a plug blocking the female's vagina. If she mates with another male, the plug stops his sperm from competing with the first male's sperm to fertilize the eggs inside her body. This way, the first male makes sure that he fathers her offspring.

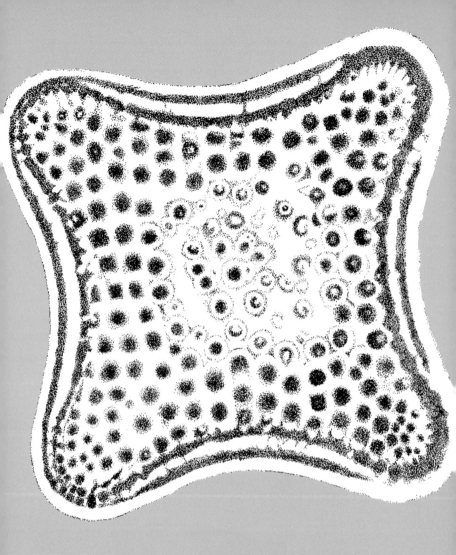

SEX **STOPS SHRINKAGE**

Diatoms are microscopic algae designed like glassy pillboxes. They divide to multiply but their average size shrinks with each generation. Then sexual reproduction steps in to save the day. Eggs fertilized by sperm produce large cells called auxospores. From these, new full-sized individuals appear. Then the divide-and-shrink process starts again.

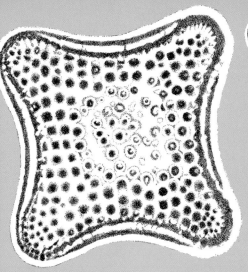
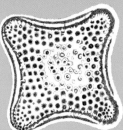
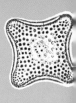

THE CHANGELING

Cuckoos dodge the hard work of raising a family. A female cuckoo adds her egg to those in the nest of a pair of small songbirds. These sit on the eggs until they hatch. The big hatchling cuckoo soon throws out the songbirds' babies. Then it gets all the food meant for them. Even when dwarfed by their adopted fast-growing child, the songbirds never notice they are feeding another bird's offspring.

GETTING ENGAGED

Two great crested grebes perform an elegant pre-mating display, spreading ear tufts and ruffs, shaking heads at each other, and preening. Then they perform "the penguin dance." Holding weed in their beaks, they tread water while raising their bodies penguinlike out of their lake to meet face to face, breast to breast. After mating they raise young on a floating nest or platform built among reeds.

SNAKE ORGY

Fresh from their winter dens, thousands of red-sided garter snakes form writhing balls of "living spaghetti." Such a mating ball forms as males try to mate with a female in the middle— or with a weak, female-mimicking, male. By surrounding himself with a living blanket, a weak male improves his chance of surviving cold and predators.

MIND THE
SPINES

"Very carefully," is the right answer to the joke question, "How do porcupines make love?" A female tree porcupine flattens her quills, raises her rear end, and brings her tail up over her back. This lays bare her spine-free genital area. If he makes the right moves, the male can then insert his penis into the female without being stabbed.

NEW FROM OLD

Sponges are primitive animals without tissues or organs yet they can reproduce in various ways: as buds that break off from a parent; as broken pieces from which new sponges grow; and as fertilized eggs from which larvae emerge. These swim around by lashing the water with "whips" before settling down on the seabed to grow.

LOBSTER LOVE

Squirting female-scented urine from a nozzle under her eyes is a female lobster's way of wooing a male in his undersea shelter. Next she moves in and shucks off her shell. Then he helps to overturn her, and with a "sex leg" thrusts a sperm packet inside her. Stored there for up to two years, the sperm will fertilize as many of the 100,000 eggs as she can lay.

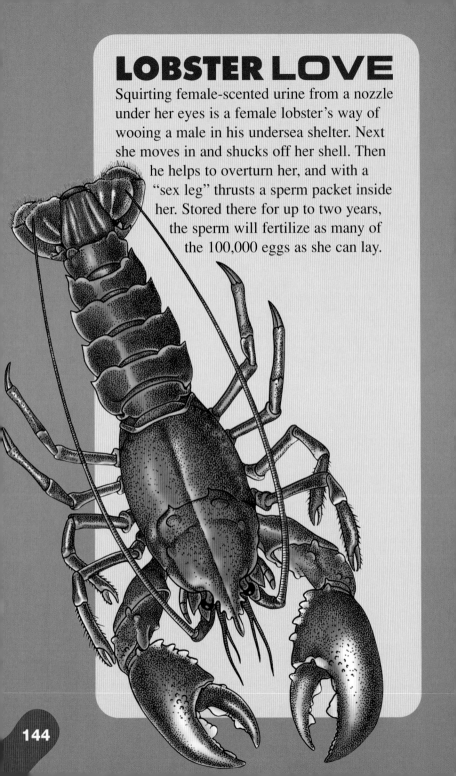

NESTING DINOSAUR

Citipati ("lord of the funeral pyre") was a dinosaur that nested on the ground, sat on its eggs, and was probably covered with feathers and down. The fossil of one found on a nest of at least 15 eggs hints that many dinosaurs courted, mated, laid eggs, brooded them, and cared for their young just like their living relatives, birds.

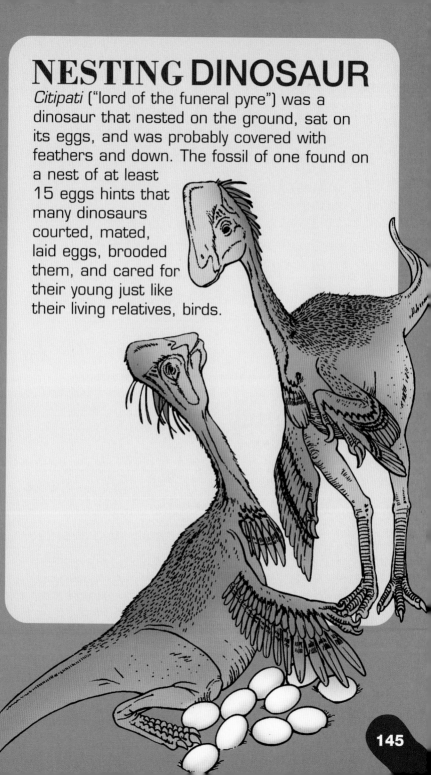

CAMEL
COURTSHIP

Courting camels often look more like enemies squaring up for a fight. The male may start by biting the female's legs, neck, and tail, and trying to pull her down. When mating begins, she lies and he sits, mounting her from behind. Then, while mating proceeds, he dribbles saliva over her while grinding his teeth.

EGGS
ON ICE

Emperor penguins breed in colonies at some of the coldest places on Earth. On sea ice stuck to Antarctica pairs bow, trumpet, and mate. Each female goes fishing after laying an egg that her partner incubates on his feet for nine weeks. Meanwhile temperatures drop to −80°F (−62°C) and winds reach 112 mph (180 kmph). Without food, males lose one third of their weight before the females return.

CUCKOO CATFISH

As a so-called mouthbrooding cichlid begins laying her eggs, a pair of cuckoo catfish zooms in and starts gobbling them up. The female catfish then lays her own eggs. Fooled into thinking they are hers, the cichlid picks them up in her mouth and broods them along with her own. The catfish eggs hatch faster than the cichlid's, whose unhatched eggs get eaten by the baby catfish.

MAGIC CICADAS

After an absence of 17 years, swarms of *Magicicada* cicadas appear. Pairs mate back to back and females then lay eggs in slits cut in trees. Their young drop off, burrow, and spend the next 16 years underground, feeding on roots. Appearing unexpectedly helps these misnamed 17-year locusts outsmart their predators.

ALL-IN-ONE SOLUTION

In lizards and other reptiles, neither sex has separate sexual organs. Instead, the sex organs are housed within the general sexual and excretory organs known as the cloaca. Once a male has joined with a female, they are firmly locked together and cannot easily be separated.

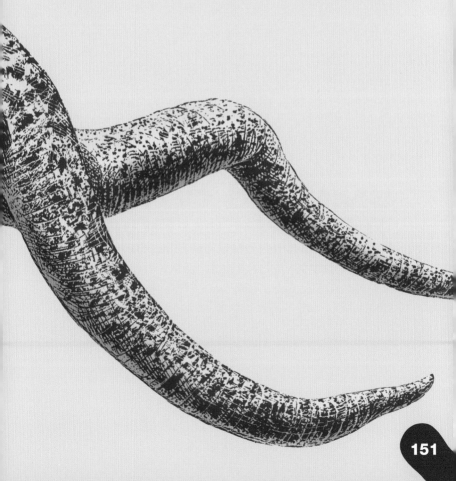

SNIFFING OUT THE OPPOSITION

Female bagworm moths leave a trail of special scent, which male bagworm moths follow. Predators of the moths—spiders—can copy the scent, so the trail may lead not to union, but to death.

BOY GIRL, GIRL BOY'

An individual oyster can change from male to female and from female to male. Each carry both eggs and sperm. They reach maturity at different times. When the sperm are ready, the oyster becomes male and releases them, and they are then sucked in by other oysters. When the eggs are ready the oyster becomes female and sucks in others' sperm. Oysters each produce up to one million eggs a year.

TALE OF
APPROVAL

Tortoises mate when the female
approves of the male by pushing
her tail out from under her shell.
During mating male rivals may try
to get under the female to tip the
lovers over onto their backs.

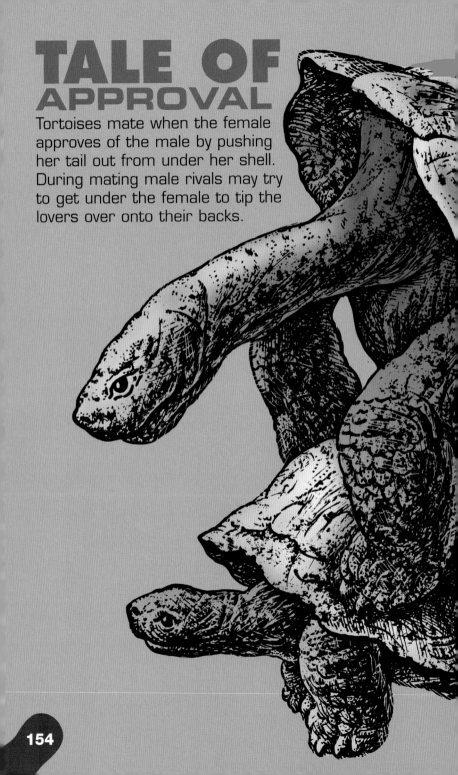

SNEAKY SUNFISH

A big male bluegill sunfish woos a female. Then she lays eggs in a nest that he guards against rival males. But medium-sized males disguised as females visit the nest, and small males quickly sneak in and out. Both fertilize some of the female's eggs without having to guard them.

TICKLING **CLAWS**

Many a male red-eared slider's courtship is a model of delicacy. Swimming to face a female, the turtle extends his forelimbs and grasps her head. Then with palms outward, he vibrates his long claws against each side of her head. If she likes this she sinks to the floor of their pond, he clambers onto her back, bends his tail beneath hers, and they mate.

HOUSE
UNDER ATTACK

Many snails have very violent mating rituals. The edible Roman snail is typical. Each individual is both male and female. At mating times, rearing up and going foot-to-foot, partners become very excited and shoot darts made of chalk into each other's bodies. Occasionally one of the snails may be stabbed to death. Finally each snail deposits its sperm in the other's bladderlike receptacle for later fertilization.

Index

INSECTS

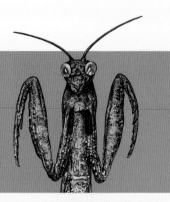

MAMMALS

REPTILES AND DINOSAURS